THERE WHERE IT'S SO BRIGHT IN ME

African
POETRY
BOOK SERIES

Series editor: Kwame Dawes

THERE WHERE IT'S SO BRIGHT IN ME

Tanella Boni

Translated by Todd Fredson
Foreword by Chris Abani

University of Nebraska Press / Lincoln

Originally published as *Là où il fait si clair en
moi* © 2017 by Éditions Bruno Doucey

Excerpts from this collection originally
appeared in *Agni*, *American Poetry Review*,
The Arkansas International, *Plume*, Poem-a-
Day, *Seedings*, and *World Literature Today*.

The University of Nebraska Press is part of a land-
grant institution with campuses and programs on the
past, present, and future homelands of the Pawnee,
Ponca, Otoe-Missouria, Omaha, Dakota, Lakota, Kaw,
Cheyenne, and Arapaho Peoples, as well as those of the
relocated Ho-Chunk, Sac and Fox, and Iowa Peoples.

♾

The African Poetry Book Series is operated by
the African Poetry Book Fund. The APBF was
established in 2012 with initial support from
philanthropists Laura and Robert F. X. Sillerman.
The founding director of the African Poetry Book
Fund is Kwame Dawes, Holmes University Professor
and Glenna Luschei Editor of *Prairie Schooner*.

Library of Congress Control Number: 2022008961

Set and designed in Garamond Premier
by Mikala R. Kolander.

To my children

Either women silence themselves,
or often they don't seem to dare say
what they are saying
—Denis Diderot

CONTENTS

FOREWORD

CHRIS ABANI

The negotiation in language, politics, history, gender, and identity is at the heart of this extraordinary translation of Tanella Boni's poetry. Rather than starting with claims, or assumptions, it questions everything. Using multiple points of view to destabilize ideas of persona, to negotiate with time and culture, to plead the case for so many transgressions, to call the reader to witness, to be implicated, to converge on realizations, even images, and metaphor, and to be moved immediately into simultaneous simultaneity, is one of the joys of the aesthetic here, and Todd Fredson's translation manages to approximate this so well and yet still lift it into transcendence.

And so, it seems that every transformational process of the African psyche is built around the motif of a journey. Not in the ways we often think of that word in modern culture, in phrases like "I am on a journey" or "this is my journey," but rather as a process of myth. Myth not in the sense of the near folkloric way it is referenced in literatures of the West, but in a still living and embodied process of becoming.

When we center ourselves in the idea of journey, as in these near throwaway new-age phrases, we lose sight of the real journey. Not one that individuates and celebrates the small will, but rather in the mythic process that brings the individual self into confrontation and negotiation with the collective self, the "mold," of the cultural person. A kind of communal individuality in which we are asked to find the balance of all our selves. To negotiate with the primordial collective human experience that underlies even the most diverse of cultures, and traditions, to ask what can belong to us, what belongs to the things bigger than us. And what obligations, oaths, and processes, bind us in a collective individuality. An interdependence that creates a holistic, healthy respect, so that we come into compliance with these conflicted selves as a series of complex choices rather than feeling shamed and coerced—a negotiation between the sacred and the mundane. In this way, in preliterate cultures, poetry has often been the vehicle for this transformation and for its transmission over time. Poets have often been the technicians of the sacred. In "Words Are My Preferred Weapons," Tanella Boni writes:

> Words are my preferred weapons
> Words that dance
> On a patch of land from which I watch
> The isthmus of my sentinel head
> Submerge in silence
> As joy spills and spills
> Across the threshold of words to come

In this deft move we see not only teleological but transformational movements. We experience home and diaspora simultaneously, we see loss and recovery at once, and we see the wholeness and holes. We see subtle allusions to work not immediately related to the subjects of Boni's work, and yet a shared history. As I read this, I was transported to another African poet, this time one of the diaspora, Lucille Clifton, who in a poem, under a tree offers libation for loss and recovery, liminal yet straddling. The journey in this, in *There Where It's So Bright in Me*, is conceptual, political, historical, metaphorical, philosophical, and yet all language and beauty. We are invited, still in the opening poem quoted from above:

Snug in my marrow this spell
Gathers my most essential baggage
I step onto other lands
Taking it with me
It never leaves me

In these modern times, where so much is assumed, so much "taken" by privilege, to ask oneself what it can mean to remain individuated and yet claimed by other selves that are public and collective is a refreshing change. Todd Fredson is becoming a reliable guide across the borders of language impeding the conversations that should be going on between African poets and readers, and poets and readers from around the world. He is doing so with care and sensitivity. Tanella Boni has published prolifically in French. We welcome such translations for what they give to us, for the way they expand the journeys of our collective selves.

TRANSLATOR'S NOTE

At Exile's Terminus

TODD FREDSON

Abroad, in the United States, Tanella Boni confronts the racialized violence that accompanies the idea of Blackness. She's arrived from West Africa, a "place that doesn't really feel / The idea's weight." Abroad, in France, a second home for Boni since her university studies, she encounters the belligerence of many Europeans as the consequences of (neo)colonialism shift the ethnic and racial profile of European citizenry, as Africans and other nonwhite migrants are viewed with skepticism.

Two civil wars between 2002 and 2011 have pushed Boni out of Côte d'Ivoire. And her returns situate her amid the extremism of al-Qaeda's Maghreb faction and the Islamic State in West Africa. Militants carried out major attacks in Ouagadougou, Burkina Faso, in Bamako, Mali, and in Grand-Bassam, Côte d'Ivoire, between January 2015 and March 2016.

The speaker in this collection wanders the once-familiar streets of her home city. She considers how, after years of exile, the names for things no longer mean what they did. She feels out where distinctions of self and other, and of belonging, are tested.

Place. Language. Personal memory. Collective memory. Has she been othered from herself? Has she been psychologically or emotionally or spiritually evicted from her home, even while the land is beneath her feet? In a body under constant threat, how does the human spirit stay buoyant? What within will guide her—what song, what radiance?

There Where It's So Bright in Me pries at the complexities of difference—race, religion, gender, nationality—that shape our twenty-first-century geopolitical conditions. The collection won the 2018 Prix Théophile Gautier from the French Academy. Across the book, Boni examines the states of exile borne out of such complexities of difference. Though, for her, as she explains in a 2019 interview, "exile" is not only physical displacement.

> *Exile* is a word I do not like very much, I've often said. You are not in exile because you are out of your home. You can be in exile at home, where you may live as a recluse, on the margins of everything. I'm not sure I've left my country. Wherever I am, it is among the baggage that I carry with me. That has always been the case. And we can see that even when I write about something else, Côte d'Ivoire does not disappear from my words.[1]

Not having language for one's experience can also become a kind of exile. This, of course, has been a central tenet of colonization—force people into colonizer languages that cannot fully render the world views, imaginations, values, beliefs, and experiences of those colonized populations. Diminish their worlds. Disappear their worlds.

Perhaps this—not having language for what one is living—has become a more generalizable circumstance, writ large by unprecedented global displacement and digital hypervisibility. We are unprepared for such sudden encounters. We don't have words for what we are seeing. We don't have expressions for the new sensory information; our own feelings seem foreign, our ideas incomplete. This is life on the doorstep of radical difference.

Still, we must find the words and expressions. We won't, Boni implies, aggress our way to understanding or reconciliation. She has titled the first section of her book "Words Are My Preferred Weapon." And across the book, using her preferred weapon, she winds her way through "extreme trials of difference."

The social, political, cultural, personal, and historicizing forces that enshroud us, what will dispel their dominions?

Is there some part of ourselves that is not bound, that is expansive beyond the confines that register our bodies? The speaker is looking out in order to witness and identify, considering how to expunge the effects of these forces. She wants to locate in herself a place from which an unconditioned address can be made, a site not marked by these wounds of circumstance. "There," she says, "where it's so bright in me."

Là où il fait si clair en moi.

Où refers equally to a place and a moment. A relative pronoun, *où* means "where," but it also means "when," indicating a place in time, a moment captured. "There," she says, "when it's so bright in me."

This time-space is luminous; it is light. But it's a pronounced light. It is clarity. And it is full of potential, potentiated, as it renews. Perhaps the lack of a comma in the title that would distinguish "there" from "where it's so bright in me" implies this active energy. There is no pause.

As the speaker says to those who would want to restrict her, good luck "[i]n the pursuit of an electron / [w]ho seeks fair exercise of the verb."

The titular space feels like tonal instruction. As the reader and as the translator I should understand this "there where" / "there when." I should ground myself in it, as the book's expression, its communication, is rooted here.

Boni has proposed a meeting place where the unconditioned address, the intention behind and within and between the words, this unique vibratory signature that is the voice of the other, might emerge. Though this other may, also, importantly, be an estranged self.

To have that presence understood, to actually feel it, is this the brightness?

This is the translation due. We recognize our limiting beliefs, those narratives we've told ourselves for temporary safety and the assumptions we've made to cover the gaps. We identify our default positions. We deconstruct our identities.

And our hearts fall to pieces. We let in a little more brightness, a little more truth. And our hearts fall to pieces. Until the myth of being whole and delineated, of being only your own, evaporates.

Witnessing the brutality garnered by Black bodies in the United States, Boni's own stories fall apart:

I have walked through the world in a dream
I didn't want to know it
I forbade myself from seeing
The actual state of it
My self-righteous speeches
Ended once I stumbled
Into this corner of the day

We may not have the words, but they are the key to something else that we have. Here is an invitation to co-create, to foster, if I were to say it, a sympathetic resonance. To be in relation without pretense. To admit an other's voice.

We are guided by a speaker who is generous and resolute.

In these poems, it feels as if Boni has unflinchingly absorbed, processed, and rendered the grief of the injustices at hand. She has not grown cold, vitriolic, or indifferent. Neither is she disaffected. The poems exhibit compassion and empathy. Her language is not delicate or precious, not heightened or overtly elegant. These poems are precise, capaciously imagined, and presented in a plain language.

Boni is one of the most prominent figures in contemporary African literature. Her work spans more than thirty-five years. Yet, only a handful of translated poems have appeared in English-language anthologies, and the first full-length collection of her poetry in translation appeared in 2018, my translation of *L'Avenir a rendezvous avec l'aube* / *The Future Has an Appointment with the Dawn*, a 2011 collection that reckons with Côte d'Ivoire's civil wars.

But, then, English-language readers rarely hear from African poets in translation, and less so from African poets who are women.

Irène Assiba d'Almeida writes in the introduction to the anthology she edited to help remediate these problems of access and representation, *A Rain of Words: A Bilingual Anthology of Women's Poetry in Francophone*

Africa (2009), that "the history of poetry published by women in francophone Africa is a very short one"—it begins in 1965. Books are published but still they "have rarely been reprinted, their poems rarely anthologized and even more rarely translated into other languages, and thus the poets receive very little critical attention."[2]

Boni's, certainly, is a voice we've been missing. And one who has already created space for us.

NOTES

1. Bios Diallo, "Tanella Boni: 'Il n'y a pas plusieurs catégories d'humains,'" *Le Point*, January 30, 2019, https://www.lepoint.fr/culture/litterature-tanella-boni-il-n-y-a-pas-plusieurs-categories-d-humains-30-01-2019-2290258_3.php#. My translation.

2. Irène Assiba d'Almeida, "Introduction, Contemporary Griottes and Stubborn Town Criers: The Making of an Anthology," in *A Rain of Words: A Bilingual Anthology of Women's Poetry in Francophone Africa*, ed. Irène Assiba d'Almeida, trans. Janis A. Mayes (Charlottesville: CARAF Books, University of Virginia Press, 2009).

THERE WHERE IT'S SO BRIGHT IN ME

Words Are My Preferred Weapons

Every departure is also a return
You leave with your dreams
You leave with life your memories
Like the slow-footed camel
You carry your baggage on your back
At the end of your arms
From stop to stop
Until the return
Your first departure
Into foreign countries

You walk down the lanes of your city
Where the trees of splendorous dreams
That shelter against the weather are rare now
In these foggy conditions the leaves
Are umbrella covers

This place seems so unfamiliar to you
Yet you are far from having failed
In some desert among giant cacti
The allure of this unknown road
Revealed no secret for you
And this face that barely recognizes you
And the rain that recalls your presence

You've always been here
But your seeing is altered
Along the way

Here is where you begin
The actual departure
It's there that the strangeness
Seizes your throat
With both hands
In the exile that begins

It will take a while
To understand
The new words
For this relation

Yet the sun is at its zenith
The sea still greets
The bay where this all began
But don't kid yourself
The neighbors' sideways looks
Tell you
That this country is far from being yours

Here you are back
More foreign than ever
This country and the air breathed
Since your departure
Has known a thousand revolutions
Seats removed each time the music stops

These are the trees that spy on your steps
But you don't have a country
Other than this one where speech came to you
As it welcomed a star's birth

You don't know when a flourishing ego
Will go off in a huff
Even as a wise word
Springs like palm sap
From your mouth

Your skin is like the tree trunk
Scored with a thousand abrasions
Protecting you again from the weather
Do you need an umbrella

Your heart may live
In the dry grass of this turmoil
Your heart that can barely accept
That a path home has opened
Charcoal still embers
In your clenched chest
Guarded by the immense silence
Of what is now unspoken in peace time

The fire that scorches your gaze
Takes you by the throat
Each time you approach
The front step

And the harmattan blows
Like a bad memory
Across these coals
Through the fragile ashes
Although the fault isn't in the weather
Blame the humans who think they are right
On a course of action
Who will not deviate one iota

It's a story without end
It wreaks havoc
Around you and in you
Does not know how to snuff
The fires eating
Ardently at the bodies

Only words will lay bare
The long walk
To that oasis
Where you'll finally satisfy your thirst

You do not have weapons other than words
Sentinels and scouts of hope
Recalling that first return
The country wrought with fear
The bitterness
The tears the uncertainty

Your horizon
Source ferrying life forward
The life the resilience
Life that rises up
Stands tall
In spite of the horrors
That people your memories
Life hope and nothing else
That's the essence of our song

I do not have another weapon in my hands
Illustrious nobody
That I never got to know
I do not have another weapon that fits me
In this hour abundant with weapons
In this world deadlocked

Words are my preferred weapons
Words that dance
On a patch of land from which I watch
The isthmus of my sentinel head
Submerge in silence
As joy spills and spills
Across the threshold of words to come

It is getting late
And time has forgotten
To join our countrysides
With happiness gone
Talk has drifted
Away from our borders

It is getting late
And I've not met you
I don't have another weapon that fits my hand

If time delivers a star to you
There among the clouds
To be counted in the evening
Pretend to see it
It is a star
A bright body
An almost-nothing
A living woman
Who knocks at your door

A woman
Never seen completely
That you must have met
In a previous life

I borrowed a quarter of the pathway
And this is where my own take their rest
Dwelling eternally
In front of the house where their words
Resonate in defiance of time
A fifty-year-old mango tree
Preserves the treasures of my memory

Here I recognize the subtlest perfume
The slightest chirping
When the sun is at its high point
The tiny music opens me to the spirit
I drink from it as if from spring water
As the storms announce themselves
And the dramatically shifting climate

This inner time is mine
Here where we meet the tiny music
Woven thread by thread
Like a handmade cotton cloth
Every plant
Every fiber finds its place
Each insect brings its song
And the weavers there at noon
The breath of the gorgeous weather

Snug in my marrow this spell
Gathers my most essential baggage
I step onto other lands
Taking it with me
It never leaves me

Whose voice is that
But mine
Slinking through
A mute world
Voice that has never told me anything more true
Than what living itself has taught me

To share the joy and pain
Of those whose voices go unheard

I don't have the chance to be a mouthpiece
My voice should have carried so far
From the rising sun
To the shadows deepening
On the edge of the night to come.

The Path of Ephemeral Lives

Who could appreciate the intensity of my voice
Me who has watched emerge a generation of ephemeral lives
Born under the sign of Color
Undesirable
Humans in their insecure
And conspicuous lives

Humans who live with peace in the soul
Without hate without grudges
Seeing straight through
Until the horizon-destroyer
Crushes their big dreams

Humans who hustle on the streets
The place reserved just for them

It's a story of here and elsewhere
A story noticeably
Written on the foreheads of travelers
Crossing borders
Even those on the right side of the law

The Other
Unstable site face of the One
But I can't imagine the uniqueness of the One
The One always various
And the Other does not see itself as the Other
Since it takes itself for the One

I'm searching for any possible meaning in the relationship
Composed via the squaring of a circle
Made by victims and aggressors
Atrocious circle shaped by hatred and rancor

I'm searching for the lucidity
That fashions doors and windows
That casts light into this trove of projections
And boxed-in dreams

Light for the ideas without wings

I'm searching for a brightness
That bursts through this clouded horizon

Next to the word *negro*
Once thrown in the face
Of those who embodied
The difference
The unseen plotter of the path
For ephemeral lives
Operates amid a thousand congested lanes

He gives himself time to trim away
These margins of the world
Probing the scribbles
Of small truths
Which are felled by some stroke
Other than common sense

For those who think they run across
His body invisible inaudible
Like a bad science-fiction film
There is nothing to see mills in the mind *what matters*
Is elsewhere

Each human guards his own dignity
It's my dignity that speaks within me

My patience lacks conviction
Me skinned alive
Shipped season to season
Day to day across the streets of the world
In the unnoticed corners

Our wise pundits forget to talk about it

Another shooting
So close to me
I'm left speechless
This voice broken
Though not astonished

I'm not talking about mass deaths
The lives cut off for nothing
I'm talking about what I see right in front of me
Indelible imprint of my skin
But this isn't really about me

I'm crossing a country sensitive
To the color of skin
I have the impression of living in the nineteenth century

A distressed humanity
Does not wait for the clarity of words
To name the unnameable

Killing in the name of difference

Skin color or the spirit in pain
The human network weakens

Simply humans

From one shooting to the next
The world unravels bit by bit

This shirking or the key to the sick game
That imperils the health of the mind
It does not take much
To lose one's bearings
In this world where such shirking
Repeats at each opportunity

Real life is permanent war
We kill at point-blank range
This is not a wail
Scattered among the clouds
That line the horizon
Of the most powerful country in the world

This shirking
Or the refusal to state
A basic truth
Which would offer a peek
At what's beneath my skin

When the shirking subsides
No one snaps awake
In the neighborhoods the houses
Nobody scrutinizes the heart of the matter
Whether there is food
On the plates
Health frays
Like a spoiled steak
This place erases
The nonexistent passengers
Arriving at their precarious jobs
The time of sobbing the long blues

The magnitude of these ephemeral lives confirms the laws

Not just a question of skin color
But of lives that must survive
Amid such stacked odds

Injustice is fashionable
In the alleys of the world
My woman's skin knows it
My steps which have come from so far away
Stumble at the borders of equality
Which is never equal in and of itself
The conditions of life forgotten
At the base of the winding staircase
Under speeches so melodious

Who opens their eyes around us
The humans excluded from the wonders
Of the human race

Who takes the time to regard
The beauty of the stars
The walker afoot
At midnight

I discover the truth of the world
Unequal
Fractured broken-down cracked
The world that I
Would never have imagined
No beauty or ugliness just transaction
I would have had so little to say
I would have written love poems
Sang the joys of living

But sometimes joy falls apart
Like butterfly wings
Gaffled in life's schemes
The joy of living batters
Against the walls
The prisons the barbed wires
That hold the names under
Until their cries
Hail death

So it dies
This relation never really figured out
Always sick with confusion
Fractured by countless misunderstandings
Because there is not enough listening
The coming together
That never takes place
Misses
What it could have been

A house is a little world
A State an entire world
And the world could have been
An uppercase world
If the hearts were not
Reservoirs of so much suffering
Bitterness
Uncertainty
That never open
To language
Until too late
When resentment
Takes possession of the spirits in distress

Losses build the world
Separations as well
While I have not gone around the world
I have traveled in me in you and you
From one border to the next
At each of my windowsills
I imagined a sailboat
So delicate in that first gust of wind

I christened the boat for crossing
Because the sea is not what one imagines
The sea in me is where I navigate
From one river to the next
Where I pass through
The most extreme trials of difference.

Memory of a Woman

I face the depths of the abyss
When the holds of the slave ships
Have disappeared from my sight
I went north to south
East to west
The cardinal points admired
The lightness of my steps
But I haven't found my country

Where had I intended to aim my boat
Now I know where I come from
Unsure of which sea I sailed
I don't move from my home
I've carried forward in my head
My memory of beautiful days
My woman's memory
Which saw everything heard everything

I approach the last bank
Serenity recovered
No dumbfounding encounters
Though nothing shocks me at this point
Life is a kingdom made beautiful by accident

Here are centuries-old palm trees
There the eucalyptuses that gnaw the soil
And the flame trees reddening in the distance
The trees do not watch one another
Even when they are neighbors
I arrive in a city full of sentinels
A city where the war has pulled apart relations

Here I am at the day's longest door
There where it's so bright in me
My reason refuses the blunt secular clarity
That separates humanity into unequal portions
Humans so divided so mistreated
And looked through
This selfhood that I've inherited
Invisible because of my skin
Which makes me so visible

This skin that has given me everything
This skin of which I'm so proud
My woman's skin that
Makes its own rules
Rules that are only a tiny part of me

I leave the question for now
My reason has half hidden the truth
That monopolized my experience as a woman

I thought I was human
Vision of such a sweet dream
Fluttering in the early gusts of wind

I wake at noon
Burnt through and through
Among my own
Who have no choice
And all the batons
That coax humanity
Into this inequality
Never equal in and of itself
Humanity so different
From the flowery idea
That protects reason

Do I want to be part of this world
Do I want to sleep soundly
Do I want to keep living
Soul tranquil heart serene

The worm's in the fruit
From the start of time
Humanity's truth is elsewhere
Here maybe
Written on skin
As if life preferred
Only a single color
In a world so diverse

The pigmentation of the skin
Requires an understanding
That continually eludes
It happens in your head

The threat
Like a flame tree
Blossoming in the shadow of the mind.

What Needs to Be Said

Reason only looks after itself
Difference is the test
The most difficult to live through
May I dare say
Without betraying what I've written

But no one wants
To hear
What needs to be said
What needs to be written
What needs to be heard
And told again like a story

Violence rolls its drums
Season after season
As if the eternal return
Was just part of these things
Planted there
Nails in our reasoning heads
These relation-devouring forces

Life is weakened
Vulnerable incomplete
Life becomes dissatisfied with being
What it is

I have walked through the world in a dream
I didn't want to know it
I forbade myself from seeing
The actual state of it
My self-righteous speeches
Ended once I stumbled
Into this corner of the day

Where the day in fact rises
And the sun shines on
The sufferings
That do not fade
The injuries
The abuse
The failures slow to scar over
The slight truth of difference
Since it must be named
Pokes into our guts with its tentacles
Slowly relentlessly
Until breathing
Is cut off
To breathe
There is only this one sacred verb
That sings with the sense of life
Those who no longer breathe are countless
And every murdered name rumbles
Thundering with media amplification
As the actual memories flake away

My skin has become
Transparent
It's undoubtedly been that way
Since the beginning
I forgot to open my eyes
Where I was
A place that doesn't really feel
The idea's weight

My neighborhood routes torn through
My speech snuffed out
My words refused
Swept under the carpet

When my boat navigates
From one sea to the other
And my skin is soaked
With the mood of the world
I find that the world prefers me
Confined to my country

Where now are my landscapes
Who cares about my home country
Who visits its side streets
Its monuments
Its beaches

Who wants me restricted to the space
Of a tribe
For the sake of authenticity
Who on my country's soil
Who at the brink of what I declare as a woman
Who wants to split me up
As if my body
Did not belong to me
Me who refuses such Stasis

I wish you much happiness
In the pursuit of an electron
Who seeks fair exercise of the verb

Here the Black lives with a belly full of fear
This fear constantly pushed back
But returned instantly to the spotlight
America in me
It is a part of my skin

The most sinuous rumor
Approaches tonight
Just outside my reach
The most sinuous rumor
Which haunts me at times

Nobody wants to hear about it
Impossible to flee
A rumor so vivid
Invisible are they
Are we

We
The mob of looked-through bodies
At which bullets are fired
Open season
It's not a rumor
I was there
Here I am

Right next to where the bullets fell
No need to be so close to the place of truth
To see the imprint of its radiance on my skin.

Might Take the Dreams as Well

A little man was sleeping in the bright sunlight
Under the gaze of a world
That had refused to see
Those faces out upon the sea of crossings

A face without any doubt
Not a bird feather an almost-nothing
Lost on the beach between two continents
An innocent face
Washed up on the beach of forgotten horrors

An angel fallen from the sky
Sleeping in the cold beneath the bright sun
Basking in that spotlight
There between the thousands of invisible countrysides
Riveted to the invisible bodies

On the unnamed sea of ancient horrors
He had a name a father an origin
A boy in the heart of a long story
Left in autumn's care

A luminous boy
A torch revealing the dark waves
Where thousands of unknown bodies
Sink silently

This symbolic image of our failing humanity
Lying on a bed of loose sand
Steps from the devouring abyss
That snatches anonymous bodies by the thousands

He bore a sharp light
He drew for a moment the eyes
Ignoring these lost dreams

They've left their countries
Hearts on their sleeves
And their blistering skin
Maintains
An indecipherable silence
Pressed against the windows
Of this grand illusion
Where the self-righteous
Cheer them with open arms

They've left their countries
On tiptoes
Countries where the cats
Grit their teeth
Against the din of disaster

The silence is perched
On mustaches
As if men
Had lost
The right way of seeing things

These things are never
Simple things
The human relationship
And the breath of love
And the time that passes
So slowly
With its stars laid
At the edge of the precipices
They have left their countries

To leave or to initiate the vital branching
But the sedentary riveted in their place
Do not hear this tiny melody
As they gather the world's money

Leaving in spite of the rain and the darkness
Heeding the horizon's call
Despite the baton and the laws

Like an insect astray
On the surface of desert dunes
Giving life to a movement taking shape

Like a crab exiled
On the high seas
Invisible to the eyes of a dubious world
Revolt worn like a sash
Over the left shoulder
Taking off without hope of return
Leaving its corner
Trusting in life
At the risk of being torn to pieces

A crustacean breathes
Until the fire gets near
Carrying it on the air to the far edge of its dreams
On alert
Until that next stop where it knows
It cannot put down roots
Because death will be near
Here or there

Suspended by the smell of evanescent dreams
You nourish the hope of postponing
That final drop
Because the day-after smiles at you
As you head
When all seems lost
To that first crossroad

The crossroad is not the hour of choice
But the way unfolding
Opening to even imperceptible breezes
To luff into the expanse does not mean losing north
It may be that the journey's trials
Expose each traveler to the extent of her purpose
The validity of her words the intensity of her speech

In the mud where the imprints
Of these ephemeral lives'
Hesitant steps
Harden
There is still nothing but pride
Out around that oasis
The freshness of rare hibiscus
A place of sand and roses

They don't want to hear
That at the end of their tireless march
Human hearts disappear
In order to let the empire of laws run its course

Flush with daylight
Their dreams have taken shape
In the dusk

With the first rays of dawn
They dress themselves in dignity with pride
They are free humans
Undertaking a journey

But the path
That their aching steps chart
Never appears
As prelude to the long march
At each door they pay
A heavy price to pass
Not sure they'll find safe harbor
Not sure they'll find
A path back

Their dreams may be confiscated
On the first step of the stairway
That leads nowhere
The stairway that can withstand any wind
While it counts
The slow turning seasons

Transparent dreams that remain unrecognizable
Like the dreams of dreamers with big dreams
When the world has turned upside down
Invisible dreams closed and flattened
Oysters unable to make a peep
Photographed as objects for the world to gawk at

They navigate they navigate
Body after starved body who emerge
Skeletons with dreams strewn piecemeal
Across some deserted beach on some shore of the world
Invisible faces bodies mummified
In these aborted dreams

Here at the crossing's midpoint
Thousands of bodies wash up
In the moonlight which weaves a shroud
In the care of smugglers handling them like stones
Ignorant of the names of these humans

Murdered by dream hunters
Buried in sea-graves
Bodies without names without markers
Only the ocean breeze to keep them company
On the first morning of the world

They don't know the throes of the sea
When night is so thick
When doors and windows
Disappear from the dimming horizon

It's a plop a simple backsplash of water
Without features without regard
It's believed that this human weight is no more than that of an idea
Anonymous thousands swallowed by the sea

Violent streams whisk the bodies
Away from the heaven of interminable debates
Among the borders and the barbed wire
That blooms unabated
At the edge of the world
Where the dugouts sleep in wrecks

They are your own people disoriented by the waves
May you never forget them

Dreams tattered but durable
Like glimmers of hope tagged to the bodies
They aren't born for the journey
The tiny branching surged deep from within their windowless isolation
There is no view of better days

They run early morning from the dry grass
Grass killed
Amassed by those entitled hands
Cunning hands that bring help
Aid that becomes a burden
No desire to reach out
When the possibility of earning a living
Fades recedes vanishes
Tiptoes away

Exile is that
A heinous word shivering down your spine
Impossible to shake
In a city of dead ends

Even caterpillars have dreams
When there is no avoiding the day's march
And the damp earth that envelops them
Marks the steps to their chrysalis

The caterpillars always have dreams
When they crawl and crawl
Before becoming butterflies

And humans too
Provided they can live them
Away from prying eyes.

Those Who Are Afraid of Naked Women

Those who are afraid of naked women
Have lost their way
And the beach wipes its tears
They believe they are right
Fighting against us all
They sew fear single-mindedly
Like dropping pebbles to keep track of their direction
In a desert they themselves have designed

Those who are afraid of naked women
Have lost the way of their Scriptures
And the beach wipes its tears
Hateful hearts
They roam
Covering their lies
In mats that they'll roll under their arms

And the beach wipes its tears
God sees all the messengers
Even the prophets
Who bury his body
In the desert
Or deep in the woods
Covered with a blood-colored shroud

Those who are afraid of naked women
Are not afraid of death
They brandish the flag
Of carefully calculated interests
They don't know the name of God
And God would not be able to identify
The blood-thirsty patrons
About whom they sing their praises

Women's faces
Steeled behind veils of constraints
Eyes brimming with naked words
Evidence of this infernal era

With each word slipped
Over that ledge of silence
Maintained with such dignity and grace
The women remember the free air
Of Timbuktu their city-memento

The oppressed nourish themselves on hope and memory
And mock these predatory laws

Dreams resist the infernal laws
That pulverize our fields of knowledge one by one
Reduce monuments to dust
Amputate the workers' hands
In shadows faces masked
Faceless faces
Stone hearts

But the dreams of the muzzled are nourished
By love and reason in the garden where sharing
Betters resistance
To all of this cruelty in the world

At these gates of the thousand silences
Hell's amputees
Remember their previous lives
In life's hard alleyways

At every step restraining themselves
Walking the rocky path of silence
Gazes lost optimistically to the horizon
They address the unrepentant predators
Through letters of labor
Written from the sweat of their brows

Who can destroy a dream
That never crumbles
Or burn memories
That always rise from the ashes

Life is not to be taken here and there
Blood is not to be spilled mindlessly
You know this very well
You who believe in your God
Which cannot be a God of hatred and death
Unless you hide some unnamed cause
In your macabre words
Just as you keep cloaked in silhouettes

We are Bassam and much more

Our lives are not Kleenex
To be tossed in the middle of the day
For your immoderate theatrics
Your world map drawn
According to the isolated flame of your bile-filled vision

We are Bassam and much more

Our lives are neither wild grasses to be torn out of the ground
Nor doormats for your macabre intentions

We are Bassam and much more

Here life smiles in the face of these fickle winds
Life that has seen so much now

We are Bassam and much more

Here life flourishes on every corner
Life that forgets hunger and being scared out of one's mind
Life that sings dances rejoices in words
Watercolor words made daily by God

We are Bassam and much more

Our God-maker-of-all-things
Far from your God-of-Terror
Sower of death blows
Accountant of mercy and malice
In the name of what do you tear
Lives from life not so easy to live with

We are Bassam and much more

On the beach of Grand-Bassam
Our city charged with history
Our country which is reborn always reborn
Impossible to line up our lives at the border
Of your blood-stained views

We are the resisters we who love life
Love and peace are our only banners

We are Bassam and much more.

The Ladder and the Spark

I don't know how to draw
But I see shapes
A square a triangle
It's a child's game
Again a circle
Within which the world is racing

I don't know how to draw
But a music haunts me
I have a bird's wing at my fingertips
I remove a feather that is eyeing me
I dip it in invisible ink
The ink that draws my presence

I found a word
That had no likeness
I did not invent it
I found it accidentally
Out on a walk

The word waved me over

I said hello to the word
Its meaning was unfamiliar
I told it that I wanted
To retrieve the images
That dwell in me and that prescribe my world

The word turned its back to me
I perceived the shape of a ladder

On the hilltop
A woman said to me
This fruit is called *kam*
Kam I take the word as it comes
I write it in my memory
Like the three letters in the word *vie**

The word gave me the key to the world
I learned to climb to the sky
Without drawing the shores
From which the sheep I imagine
Drown themselves in the sea

Since that time
I've been drawing ladders
A child's game
To keep the world
At your fingertips
And I dream that I am a poet
But I don't know

---

* *Vie* means life, but *kam* is an untranslatable word, perhaps a sacred word, so adding a
fourth letter to *kam* in order to match the four letters in the translation of *vie* to "life"
feels inappropriate. I leave *kam* and *vie* as I find them.

If there was no river to cross
Its music would be missing from the world
If there was no salt in the ocean
There'd be no poems

Take the music as it comes
Staccato rhythmic melodic
It is jazz and a balafon
It is drum and trombone
And the flute that makes a bouquet of our emotions
When the music softens
And the words flit from one world to the next
Life is like that never monotone

Love is born from headwinds
To better align
Our incompatible moods

The depth of blackness
Illuminates those looks
Frozen in old panes
Nothing filters through them
The louvers that let air in are gone
Leaving the wooden frames but no horizon

This corseted thought
Resembles
The ready-to-wear opinions
Trending so loudly
In the public square

You search for the breeze
That persists regardless of the season
You don't perceive it yet
The windowpanes slump and shift
According to the sway of whatever words sell at the moment

With each step you hope
To progress against that distant horizon
You cross the almighty emptiness
That hangs its honeycomb suites
Far from any shared shoreline

The sea of discourse is so difficult
To cross

Among the words and the verbs
Of political discourse
The price of honey climbs

The foraging bees
Near the best nectar
Take flight in swarms
They are nomadic
A species of insect
That seems to prosper in Africa

Their essential
The worship of appearances
And who cares anyway about those discordant voices
Counting the stars
At the feet of humans
Going through hell
Living hand to mouth

Let me add a warning to those of you
Who know how to make your own honey
Blossom right from your pores
Honey day and night

Those guardians of walls and enclosures
Despise your air of freedom
They are watching your eyes scan the distance
They are shadowed and masked

Here or there
They watch you thread
Time's colors
They scrawl your woman's steps
Across that place's walls

They say that you attract
The storms
But it's not heaven's tears
That kill time's body
On your skin you print
The world's mood
And the time-spirit
Awake in you

The sea's clock
Doesn't mark inner time with words

In reality you have left the noise of the city
Where the cats transform
Into spotted hyenas without even knowing

Let things unfold casually
The horizon fixes your gaze
And the invisible source of dreams
Takes you by the hand
You are deep in the forest
The kapok trees do not know your name
But the wild grasses
Welcome your steps with joy
Between strides
They see the world at your feet

In the world of small things
A good fire costs nothing
It burns it heats
Love is worth every gold piece on this planet

Spark a light in the corner of your eye
And cross the humanless void of desert
As if life were flourishing
At every door and window

Forgo the rules
Of this impersonal world
Whose violence is crushing
Your frail presence
Don't wait for the flame
To go out in you.

Eight New-Generation African Poets: A Chapbook Box Set
Edited by Kwame Dawes
and Chris Abani
(Akashic Books)

New-Generation African Poets: A Chapbook Box Set (Tatu)
Edited by Kwame Dawes
and Chris Abani
(Akashic Books)

New-Generation African Poets: A Chapbook Box Set (Nne)
Edited by Kwame Dawes
and Chris Abani
(Akashic Books)

New-Generation African Poets: A Chapbook Box Set (Tano)
Edited by Kwame Dawes
and Chris Abani
(Akashic Books)

New-Generation African Poets: A Chapbook Box Set (Sita)
Edited by Kwame Dawes
and Chris Abani
(Akashic Books)

New-Generation African Poets: A Chapbook Box Set (Saba)
Edited by Kwame Dawes
and Chris Abani
(Akashic Books)

New-Generation African Poets: A Chapbook Box Set (Nane)
Edited by Kwame Dawes
and Chris Abani
(Akashic Books)

To order or obtain more information on these or other University of Nebraska Press titles, visit nebraskapress.unl.edu. For more information about the African Poetry Book Series, visit africanpoetrybf.unl.edu.

Printed in the USA
CPSIA information can be obtained
at www.ICGtesting.com
LVHW090739290124
770114LV00041B/446